Caroline E.R. Parker

The Old Kitchen Fire, and Other Poems

Caroline E.R. Parker

The Old Kitchen Fire, and Other Poems

ISBN/EAN: 9783337256371

Printed in Europe, USA, Canada, Australia, Japan

Cover: Foto ©Thomas Meinert / pixelio.de

More available books at **www.hansebooks.com**

THE
OLD KITCHEN FIRE,
AND
OTHER POEMS.

BY

MRS. CAROLINE E. R. PARKER.

PUBLISHED BY THE
AMERICAN TRACT SOCIETY,
150 NASSAU-STREET, NEW YORK.

CONTENTS.

THE OLD KITCHEN FIRE, AND OTHER POEMS.

THE OLD KITCHEN FIRE.

Oh, happy were my early days,
  And pleasant was my home,
And sunny was the green hillside,
  Where I once loved to roam.
But ah, no scene can I recall,
  My thoughts with joy t' inspire,
Compared to my own little seat
  Beside the kitchen fire.

The quiet winter evening,
  When with my simple book
Or knitting-work, I claimed my seat
  In that snug, cosy nook:

I listened to the older folk,
For I could never tire
Of all the twice-told tales I heard
Beside that kitchen fire.

The spacious chimney, deep and wide,
The broad old kitchen hearth
Of bright-red bricks, which in the blaze
Would blink, as if in mirth.

The kettle sending forth its steam,
  And cheery little song,
The low, calm ticking of the clock,
  Speeding the hours along.

The cricket, from its hiding-place
  His chirping song would lend,
With merry heart, I welcomed him
  As if he were a friend.
The smiling basketful of chips
  Did screen the little thing ;
I did not care to hunt him out,
  I 'd rather hear him sing.

And pussy sat, with half-shut eyes,
  And black and glossy fur,
Dozing the sleepy hours away
  With low, contented purr.
How the great logs would blaze and roar,
  And crackle as they lie ;
While the bright sparks went trooping up,
  A goodly company.

I used to wonder at the crane
  Which stretched its blackened arm
Across the fire, in giant strength
  Boldly defying harm.
Trammels and hooks my wonder were,
  Suspended link by link ;
That dear romance was long since lost
  In copy-books and ink.

What magic power that bright fire had;
No artist ever drew
With skilful hands such glowing scenes,
All beautiful and new.
Bright colors from dear fairy land
The happy limner blends,
And mid the embers shadows forth
Faces of little friends.

Old happy times! my heart goes back
And wonders at the change,
While painful memories press around,
And whisper—is it strange?
"Oh, where has gone the simple heart,
The humble, calm desire
Which made that little seat so dear,
Beside that kitchen fire?"

THE DEATH-WATCH.*

Tick on, tick on, sad monitor,
In the silent hush of night;
Within my chamber wall I heed
Thy tapping, low and light.

* This ticking is made by a small beetle, an insect with shelly wings, and is really the call of the male insect to its mate, sometimes weakly supposed to prognosticate death. WEBSTER'S DICTIONARY.

Close to my ear thy warning voice,
  Tick, tick, it sayeth plain;
I turn to seek thee, little thing,
  But turn and seek in vain.

Tick on, tick on, sad little voice,
  A warning thou mayest be;
Telling, perchance, the angel Death
  Is keeping watch for me,

And kindly placed this monitor
  Within my quiet room,
To count for me the few brief hours
  Between me and the tomb.

Tick on, tick on, kind little voice,
  Thy lesson I would learn;
Nor from my heart in cold contempt
  The simple teacher spurn.

"Be ready," saith the little voice,
  "Whene'er thine hour shall come;
Or soon or late, thy Master sends
  To call thy spirit home.

"Oh, fear me not, nor shrink with dread
  When my small voice you hear;
'Be ready' is the warning word
  I whisper in thine ear.

"Tick, tick, thy moments fly apace,
  Thy life, so short at best,
Watch well, to-night thou mayest be called
  Unto thy better Rest."

THANKSGIVING DAYS.

GLAD days, sad days, my heart can hardly tell
Whether to joy or sigh at the return
Of this home festival, remembered well
From earliest childhood, though I can discern
Deep cause for thankfulness towards that Hand
Which doth our harvests send, our garners fill,
And scattereth "perfect gifts" throughout the land;
And yet the burden of my heart is still,
Glad days, sad days.

Glad days, glad days, for round the social board
The best belovèd of our hearts we meet;
With many a pleasant smile and cheerful word
The happy family each other greet.
And childhood's merry laughter hails the cheer,
And quiet matrons look approving on;
Or joining in the sports with those so dear,
They thus recall their youth for ever flown.
Glad days, glad days.

Sad days, sad days, the weary heart goes back
And counts its treasures now for ever fled,
And sigheth, as upon its silent track
It doth recall sweet faces of the dead.
More than the living the departed are,
The grave claims more than meet around our hearth,
And oh, the mem'ry of the loved and fair
Comes like a shadow o'er our social mirth;
Sad days, sad days.

Glad days, sad days; deem not the loved ones gone,
Or absent from us at this hallowed hour,
Though from our side they seem for ever flown,
They still are with us, and we feel their power.
The youth, the matron, and the little child,
The aged parent, and the maiden fair
Smile on us now, as long ago they smiled.
Save now, no shade of sorrow or of care,
Sweet voices, made more sweet by angel's songs,
Whisper to us of our eternal rest,
None absent, no, not one, a goodly throng,
Thrice welcome to our hearts these angel guests;
Glad days, sad days.

THE SILVER MOON.

ART peeping in my window now,
Thou shining silver moon,
And lighting up with thy soft rays
My quiet little room!

Oh, tell me, tell me, what fair things
Thou seest from yon height,
While thus thou lookest down on earth
Throughout this summer night;

Shining upon the broad hillside,
And peeping into bowers,
Lighting the tree-tops green and tall
And looking after flowers—

Thou 'lt find the violet's blue eye shut,
The roses fast asleep,
And daisies nodding in their dreams
Beneath the verdant steep.

Thou 'lt peep into the little nests
Of birds safe in the tree,
And blackbird, sparrow, linnet, thrush,
And sleeping robin see.

Thou 'lt look down in the waters clear,
And spy the fishes bright,
Still on the pebbly sand asleep,
Through the long, pleasant night.

Thou peepest in my little room;
I open wide my eyes,
And hail thee as a pleasant friend,
With joy and glad surprise.

I thank the Lord who made thee shine,
And blessed me with thy light;
Then close my eyes, and dream of thee,
Fair silver moon, good-night.

TO A ROBIN IN WINTER.

WHY dost thou tarry here, poor bird?
The winter has begun,
The clouds are thick and dull and gray,
And hidden is the sun.
Hie, hie
Unto some summer sky;
Now come,
Till warmer days return.
Come listen, and my pleasing word,
I prithee, do not spurn.

I thank you for your company,
And greet your cheerful song;
With grateful heart, dear little bird,
I 'd listen all day long.
But no,
The chilling wind doth blow.
I 've heard
That like brave Robin Hood,
Thou hast a shelter warm and dry,
Far in the close, green wood.

Ah, like a friend most kind and true,
I know that thou wilt come
Even in the darkest winter days,
To cheer my lonely home.
Kind bird,
Thy little chirping word
I praise.
Most gentle is thy tone,
Come, robin, with the chosen few,
And share my cheerful home.

Thou wilt not come? dost thou mistrust
My very kindliness?
I have no truer wish, poor thing,
Than thy small self to bless;
I'll warm
Thy pretty little form,
And sing
Sweet songs into thy ear,
And give thee crumbs, if thou wilt trust
Thyself unto my care.

Ah, no. For there is One above
Who careth much for thee;
Who bade thee linger in the woods
Though other songsters flee.
And finds
Thee shelter from the winds
And food;

And tunes thy cheerful voice
To cheer us with its lays of love,
And make our hearts rejoice.

CHILDHOOD.

THE smiles of blessed childhood,
How much of joy they tell;
Gushing unbidden, warm and free
From out the heart's glad well.
Telling of fountains filled with joy,
Of pleasures new and fair;
Scattering their cheerful influence
Like sunbeams everywhere.

The tears of April childhood
Still glisten as they rise,
Reflecting back in rainbow hues
Bright colors from the skies.
For clouds pass lightly o'er the heart,
Like shadows o'er a lake;
So grief upon the guileless soul
Can no sad impress make.

The sports of merry childhood,
The joyous laugh and bound,
The gladsome shout that fills the air,
And echoes round and round;

The healthful sport, the quiet games,
  The rambles far and wide
For flowers in summer, or the tale
  By winter's glad fireside.

The sleep of sunny childhood,
  How kindly doth it come;
Rest for the child, as for the flower
  When summer day is done.
In fairy land of pleasant dreams
  Roameth the sleeper dear;
And smiles light up the silent face,
  As angels whisper near.

The prayer of trusting childhood,
  That simple, earnest faith
Which yieldeth to a Father's care
  The care of all it hath;
Which asketh—and receiveth
  Because no doubts arise
But what its simple wishes reach
  "Our Father" in the skies.

The death of happy childhood,
  While day has but begun,
To see the glorious rising
  Of another brighter sun;
To pass away ere sorrow comes
  With her chill, withering hand;
Fresh, as from God, to pass away
  Into the better land.

The grave of peaceful childhood,
  Grass-grown, and fair to see,
Watched by affection's loving eye,
  And guarded carefully.
At eventide the daisies sleep
  Upon the quiet bed;
While in far deeper slumber rests
  The young, the cherished dead:

The heaven of ransomed childhood:
  O Lamb of God once slain,
"The little ones" thou lovest still,
  All worthy is thy name!
In bright array they gather round
  Thy throne of light divine;
Safe in thy love, no more to roam,
  Dear Saviour, they are thine.

Spring Flowers.

How beautiful are flowers! oh, I love
  In early Spring to watch their coming up,
And over hill and dale how sweet to rove,
  To greet the opening of the earliest cup.

They seem to me like children young and fair,
  Gentle and trusting, and as such I fain
With kindly welcome go to meet them where
  God sends on them his sun and gentlest rain.

Oh, I go forth to meet them with a heart
  Full of warm gratitude that they thus come
In simple loveliness to do their part
  In making glad my temporary home.

They lay so gladsomely along the way,
  Like smiles upon a green and sunny bank,
In beautiful confusion, or arrayed
  In marshalled order, a fair floral rank.

God of the Spring, thou scatterest many flowers
  To cheer us pilgrims on our weary way;
Oh, may they teach us of the hope that 's ours,
  Of cloudless skies and never-ending day.

THE LADY ALICE.

A SONG.

Art dreaming, Lady Alice?
  With thy gentle, downcast look;
Oh, let thy quiet beauty be
  Unto my heart a book;
And I will read its pages
  As I gaze upon thy face,
And in each perfect lineament
  A hidden meaning trace.

Art dreaming, Lady Alice?
  No sorrow in thy gaze;
Thy blue eyes' radiant lustre,
  And thy hair like golden rays.

Thy snowy bosom heaveth;
  But grief is not a guest
Within the peaceful shelter
  Of that gentle maiden's breast.

Art dreaming, Lady Alice?
  The future seemeth bright;
And down its opening vista
  A line of golden light.
Oh, happy, happy summer time
  Of love, and joy, and truth,
When loving hearts trust loving hearts
  With simple, earnest truth.

Art dreaming, Lady Alice?
  There may come at last a day
When from thy day-dreams beautiful
  The light may fade away.
When clouds may dim the summer morn,
  And tears may dim thine eye,
And youth, and hope, and promised joys
  All cold and silent lie.

Art dreaming, Lady Alice?
  Trust not to earth alone;
There are living waters flowing
  Fast by the great white throne.
Seek thou those living waters,
  Seek thou that throne of God
In youth, that happy summer-time,
  Seek thou his blest abode.

OUR FATHER, WHO ART IN HEAVEN.

THY Father, little one, and mine,
  Is he who reigns above ;
Thy prayers and mine he deigns to hear
  In mercy and in love.
Thy prayers and mine, dear little child,
  He deigns in love to hear ;
Oh, to his blessed mercy-seat
  Let us in faith draw near.

Thy Father, little one, and mine ;
  All hallowed be his name ;
Oh, pray thou that his will be done
  In earth and heaven the same.
Thy Father, little one, and mine,
  Pray thou for daily bread ;
For by his power alone we live,
  And by his bounty fed.

Thy Father, little one, and mine :
  Forgive, and be forgiven ;
That ye may worthy followers be
  Of Him who reigns in heaven.
Thy Father, little one, and mine :
  Temptations peep around ;
Oh, pray, lest you be left to tread
  Upon unhallowed ground.

Thy Father, little one, and mine;
From evil keep us, Lord;
Oh, turn our feet in those blest paths
That lead thee to our God.
Thy Father, little one, and mine;
To him the glory be;
To him the kingdom, him the power
To all eternity.

"Clothed Upon."

2 CORINTHIANS 5:2.

Our "earthly house" must pass away,
This tabernacle frail though fair,
Made in the image of its God,
And fashioned with such wondrous care.

This frame, so wrought with perfect skill,
With seeing eye and hearing ear;
With busy hands and restless feet,
With life-blood flowing warm and clear;

"Our earthly house must be dissolved;"
The restless foot no more to rove;
The busy hands must cease from work;
The throbbing heart forget to move;

And then we shall be "clothed upon;"
"We have a house not made with hands"
Built by our God, eternal, fixed,
Sure as his word of mercy stands.

Oh, not "unclothed," but "clothed upon,"
This mortal shall immortal be;
Life shall be swallowed up of life
When Jesus sets the spirit free.

Building of God! be mine the prize!
Yes, "clothed upon" with his dear love,
Safe in the sheltering of that home
My wandering feet no more will rove.

Yes, "clothed upon," oh gracious word;
Clothed in his vesture pure and white,
"For ever present with the Lord,"
And dwelling in eternal light.

BLUE FLOWERS.

You ask which flowers I love the best
When Spring calls forth her pretty train,
And each in cheerful garments dressed
She sends them forth o'er hill and plain!
Give me blue flowers
To grace my bowers—
"The perfect color," heaven's own blue;
Meek violet
In emerald set,
And glistening with the fragrant dew;
Or by the brook
With downcast look,

The nodding harebell's fairy form
I love to see,
Where lowly she
Doth bend her head to meet the storm.

Blue flowers, oh, give me fair blue flowers!
So pleadingly their azure eyes
Uplook in mine at morning hour,
Taking their color from the skies.
Of heaven they burn,
To heaven they turn
Their opening bells at break of day;
And heaven doth shed
On each fair head
A blessing on them where they lie;
A blessing meet
For flowers so sweet,
A portion of her glory bright;
Our prayer should be,
Oh, thus may we
Be clothed upon with robes of light.

NIGHT.

'TIS holy night! the stars are out
Upon their watches far on high;
The moon's slight shell upon the edge
Of the horizon's verge doth lie,

Looking a fair "Good-night" to me
Who watch her course thus silently.

'Tis holy night! the moon hath gone
With timid steps to seek her lord;
The sun her master is, and she,
Ever with loving sweet accord,
Through night and day doth follow him,
Lest her pale light should grow more dim.

'Tis holy night! God grant that I
A lesson from its page may know;
Just like the moon, through night and day,
Through present joy and coming woe,
My Lord's dear face to keep in view,
And follow him with worship true.

May I, with meek and lowly heart
  Follow *my* Lord with trusting love,
Keeping an eye, undimmed and clear,
  Upon his glory far above;
For, like the moon's, must grow
  My light and life if far from Him.

"Standing Idle."

MATTHEW 20:3.

Standing idle in the market
  When the Lord hath work to do;
See, his vineyard needeth tending,
  Room to work for me and you.

Oh, go forth, 'tis early morning,
  "Work to-day," the Master saith;
Train the fragile vines and tendrils,
  Work in patience, work in faith.

Standing idle at the noontide,
  See, the Master draweth nigh;
"Go ye also in my vineyard,
  Work, for yet the sun is high."

Standing idle, shades of even
  Gather over hill and plain;
Yet go forth, go forth to labor,
  While the light of day remains.

Work for all in His great vineyard ;
None too feeble, none too weak,
But the Master finds some duty,
If his blessed work we seek.

Standing idle, while one sinner
Lives to heed a warning voice ;
While to one afflicted brother
We can say, "Poor heart, rejoice."

Oh, go forth with strong endeavor,
Now to do your Master's will ;
'Tis to-day he calls his laborers,
Oh, his earnest work fulfil.

And when even comes, the Master
Gives each laborer his reward ;
May we feel the blest assurance,
Faithfully we 've served our Lord.

TRUST IN GOD.

"Not what I will, but what thou wilt." MARK 14 : 36.

"NOT what I will, my Father," be my prayer,
Whate'er my lot on earth, in joy or woe,
Thy will, not mine, in all things here below.
When all seems bright and heaven is smiling fair,
And my heart feels no weight of grief or care,
Then 't is, thy will, my Father, makes me blest ;
And I, with grateful heart to thee repair,
To thank thee for the hours of peace and rest.

And when dark clouds o'ershadow my bright sky,
And anguish wrings my soul—oh, then, my heart,
From thy firm trust in God do not depart.
"Not what I will, my Father," be my cry,
"Thou knowest best—let me thy love descry;"
'T is the same Hand dispensing good and ill,
All good, though seeming ill to mortal eye.
This wish alone my inmost being fill,
"Just what thou wilt, my Father," be my will.

The Autumn Leaves

Oh! come, let us gather the Autumn leaves,
Here are brown, and bright yellow and red,
Let us choose a snug spot, close up by the hedge,
And make us a nice little bed.
Come, Jennie, come Lizzie, come gather the leaves,
The beautiful autumn leaves.

Here are yellow, they come from the great elm-tree,
And brown from the beech hard by,
And the glowing red and the orange bright
From the maple-tree so high;
Come Jenny, come Lizzie, come gather the leaves,
The beautiful autumn leaves.

How brilliant they are! with the sunset hues
The trees seemed tinged as they stand,
They look like the pictures of "golden trees"
We read of in fairy land.

Come Jenny, come Lizzie, come gather the leaves,
 The beautiful autumn leaves.

And the children there in their merry sport
 Did gather the leaves as they fell,
And made a fair bed of the fragrant heap
 Close down in the sheltered dell;
They gathered the leaves as they fell from the trees,
 The beautiful autumn leaves.

I looked in the face of sweet Nelly my pet,
As she heaped up treasures fair,
And her eye was bright, and her lip was red,
And curly her sunny hair;
And she sang as she gathered the leaves as they fell,
The beautiful autumn leaves.

And I thought of an eye, as bright as hers
That was closed in its last long sleep,
And a little foot, and a merry voice
That was hushed in slumber deep;
And the autumn leaves lay thick on her grave,
The beautiful autumn leaves.

And I spoke to the children one and all
Of the grave by the willow-tree,
And they clustered around me with earnest gaze
These lovely children three,
As the autumn leaves lay scattered around,
The beautiful autumn leaves.

And I led them close to the quiet grave,
And the autumn leaves were there;
And they covered the dead, in her little bed,
With a draping rich and rare;
They lay like a garment upon the spot,
The beautiful autumn leaves.

And in accents low, I spoke to the three
Of the little slumberer there:
"Last autumn she gathered the leaves as they fell,
And thought they were passing fair;

She gathered the leaves as they fell from the trees,
The beautiful autumn leaves.

"She loved the Lord when a little child,
The good Lord called her home;
And she faded away like the autumn leaves,
When a chilling frost comes on—
Like the autumn leaves she faded away,
The beautiful autumn leaves.

"And we laid her away in this quiet nook,
Our Mary so gentle and fair;
But in faith we point to a better land
For we know that her spirit is there;
Though the leaves lie thick on her little grave,
The beautiful autumn leaves.

"The leaves teach a lesson we all must learn,
We all 'do fade as a leaf;'
Oh, love the Lord in your early youth,
For life at best is brief.
The leaves teach a lesson we all must learn,
The beautiful autumn leaves."

Then we gathered the leaves that lay scattered around
And covered the little bed,
And we kneeled in prayer in that quiet spot
Close, close by the sleeper's head.
And the leaves lay thick on that little grave,
The beautiful autumn leaves.

"LORD, IS IT I?"

MATT. 26:22.

LORD, is it *I?* I ask in tears and sadness,
I, thy disciple, at thy sacred board,
Who from thy cup have drank, thy bread have broken,
Oh, is it *I* who shall betray my Lord?

"Lord, is it I?" I ask in deep emotion.
"Exceeding sorrowful," my heart would say,
"Though I should die with thee, I'd not deny thee;
Forbid it, Lord, that I my trust betray."

"Lord, is it I?" Thou knowest that I love thee;
I love thy habitation, and thy seat,
I love to hear thy gospel's holy teachings,
With Mary I would worship at thy feet.

"Lord, is it I?" I tremble at the question;
Oh, is my faith so weak in Christ my God,
That I for worldly gain could sell my Master,
That I for worldly gain deny my Lord?

"Lord, is it I?" Thou knowest my temptations,
My spirit willing, though the flesh is weak,
My earnest striving, and my often failing,
Sinning, repenting, still thy grace I seek.

"Lord, is it I?" Oh, cheer my drooping spirit;
Unto thy cross I cling in humble prayer,
Distrusting all but thee, and thy great mercy;
O blessed Saviour, take me in thy care.

THE SKY-LARK.

GOD speed thee, little wanderer!
Wherever thou art flying,
On swift wing far above my head
Thy little form has upward sped
And upward still is hieing!
Dear little bird! how sweet to gaze,
As thou art high ascending,
And up in many a mystic maze
Thy heavenward path art wending.

God bless thee, little wanderer!
Singing as up thou soarest;
With joy I hear the silver note,
That sweetly from thy little throat
So thankfully thou pourest.
Dear little bird, how sweet to hear,
As thou art high ascending,
Thy happy song, while cheerily thou
Thy heavenward path art wending.

God grant me, lowly wanderer,
  A spirit ever winging
An upward flight—nor stooping save
To plume her wing, and freely lave
  In founts eternal springing;
And give me heart *to sing*, as I
  My heavenward path am wending,
Singing and soaring till my voice
  With angels' songs is blending.

Resurrection Morning.

"And when the Sabbath was past, Mary Magdalene, and Mary the mother of James, and Salome, had brought sweet spices, that they might come and anoint him. And very early in the morning, the first day of the week, they came unto the sepulchre at the rising of the sun." St. Mark 16: 1, 2.

Very early in the morning,
  When the Sabbath-day was done,
Came the holy women sadly,
  Ere the rising of the sun;
Came they to the silent garden,
  And within the solemn shade
Sought the sepulchre of Joseph,
  Where their blessèd Lord was laid;
    Very early.

Very early in the morning,
  With sad hearts and weary feet,
To anoint the Saviour's body
  Came they there with spices sweet.

As they journey, midst their weeping
  Hear them to each other say,
"From the door securely guarded
  Who shall roll the stone away?"
            Very early.

Very early in the morning
  Angels rolled away the stone,
And within the tomb of Joseph
  Heavenly brightness round them shone.
But the holy women wondering,
  Midst their tears thus sadly say,
"Oh, we know not where they've laid Him,
  They have taken him away,
            Very early."

Very early in the morning
  Meet they there their risen Lord,
Blessèd Mary first to greet him,
  Christ, their Saviour and their God.
Forth to tell the glorious tidings
  Haste they from the tomb's dark prison;
Listen to the wondrous story,
  "Christ the Lord indeed is risen,
            Very early."

Very early in the morning
  Children come with incense sweet,
Humble prayers and joyful praises,
  Glad hosannas to repeat.

Very early in the morning
  Children, in glad choruses,
Join the Marys, and proclaim it,
  "Christ the Lord is risen to-day,
          Very early."

LINES.

Lady, oh do not turn away,
  Whene'er I meet your eye;
You know not how I love to gaze
  On its soft brilliancy;
The melting blue, that lies half hid
  Beneath that lash of jet,
Tells me of one I weep for still,
  But never can forget.
So, lady, may I sometimes gaze
On beauty that I dare not praise?

That full red lip is so like hers,
  And thy soft, shining hair
Like folded sunbeams shades a brow
  As fair as hers was fair.
That smile, so like my loved one's smile,
  That voice whose every tone
Recalls the music of a voice
  I almost called my own—
'T is a sad joy to gaze on thee,
Lady, turn not away from me.

THE NEW MOON.

"The young moon
Upon the sunlit limits of the night." SHELLEY.

GOD bless thee, lovely wanderer!
Welcome, fair queen of night!
Thy sunlit eye so softly beaming,
Over my pathway sweetly gleaming,
So like a blessed guardian seeming—
God bless thy gentle light.

God bless thee, lovely wanderer!
How have I longed for thee;
When lo, to-night I turned my eye,

And there hung up in the blue sky
Thy lovely form I did descry,
A welcome sight to me.

God bless thee, lovely wanderer!
Thy light doth cheer my heart;
A sweet companion thou to me,
A blessed sight for me to see,
A friend whose pleasant company
Doth ever peace impart.

God bless thee, lovely wanderer!
How happy should I be,
If ever through life's varied way
Some friend like thee could cheer each day,
Some beaming smile like thy soft ray
Could ever comfort me.

"In Thy Good Time."

In thy good time, dear Lord, in thy good time
I shall find rest,
Far from the strife and tumult of the world,
In regions blest.

After the heat and turmoil of the day,
The quiet night
With fragrant breeze, while silver stars look down
With softened light.

After the heat and burden of life's day,
The quiet grave;
Rest for the wearied frame and aching heart
Where sweet flowers wave.

After the storm upon the billowy deep,
The gentle calm;
Fierce winds are hushed, and soothing gales steal down,
Like healing balm.

After the storms upon life's billows deep
I shall find peace—
That blessed peace, in realms of holy joy,
Where sorrows cease.

In patience, Lord, I wait for thy good time,
When thou wilt come
To take me to my everlasting rest,
My heavenly home.

ARE THEY SINGING SONGS AT HOME?

A SONG.

ARE they singing songs at home
In our cottage by the sea,
As once in the days long past
They sang those songs with me?

At the quiet eventide,
  Though a wanderer far and lone,
Oft my heart the question asks,
  "Are they singing songs at home?"

Are they gathered round the fire,
  In our cottage by the sea,
Talking of old happy times,
  Just as once they talked with me?
Does the merry laugh ring out?
  Do the children shout and play?
Though alone in distant lands
  I'm a wanderer far away.

Do they kneel at evening hour,
  In our cottage by the sea?
Do they pray with simple faith,
  Just as once they prayed with me?
Does the quiet, calm "good-night"
  Fall from lips I love so well,
While, with weary, weary heart,
  In sad loneliness I dwell?

Let them sing the dear old songs
  In our cottage by the sea;
Let them gather round the fire,
  For they'll think and talk of me
Let the simple evening prayer
  On the wings of faith ascend;
For I know, at the throne of grace,
  My name with theirs will blend.

Tares and Wheat.

Standing together, side by side,
  Tares and wheat, in the Master's field.
Each with its blade of shining green,
  Each with its grain in its silken shield.

The wheat was sowed by the Master's hand.
  The seed was good, and sowed with care;
But while men slept in the summer night,
  An enemy came and scattered tares.

Side by side in the cheerful sun,
  Each refreshed by the soft'ning shower;
Alike they wave in the balmy breeze,
  And bend their heads in the evening hour.

Waiting together till harvest-time,
  Tares and wheat in the Master's field,
The reaper comes with his sickle keen,
  And each to his shining blade must yield.

Cast forth the tares, in the fire to burn;
  But saith the Master, in accents sweet,
"Into my barns with thanksgiving and joy
  Gather my beautiful golden wheat."

Ah, thus in our Master's harvest-field,
  The wheat and tares grow side by side;
He sendeth his sun, he sendeth his rain,
  Blessings he scattereth far and wide.

At last he sendeth his reaper forth—
His reaper Death, with his sickle keen;
And he gathers the beautiful golden wheat,
And the worthless tares that grow between.

Oh, patient soul in the harvest-field,
Wait, oh, wait till the Master come;
He knoweth his wheat from the enemy's tares,
His own will he bear to his harvest home.

"There Remaineth therefore a Rest."

Lonely and sad, my spirit often turns
Her tearful eyes to heaven's eternal rest,
And like a dove, whose wearied pinions yearn
For the safe shelter of her little rest,
My heart doth sigh,
Oh, could I find
At last like wearied dove
A shelter from the wind.

My spirit full of hope goes forth at morn,
Nerved for the duties of the coming day;
But soon she wearies of her purpose strong,
And oftentimes she fainteth by the way,
O'ercome by grief,
By care oppressed,
With little strength to bear,
She longeth for her rest.

My spirit oftentimes doth visions see
  Of dear departed ones long gone before—
Ever belovèd, and they beckon me
  To join their hosts, and with them heavenward soar
      My wingless soul
        Would fain arise;
      But pinions doth she lack
        To bear her to the skies.

My soul would not repine, I am content
  To wait till Christ sees fit to call me home;
But very lonely, and with toil o'erspent,
  I'm daily longing for the rest to come—
      Her staff in hand,
        Without the gate,
      A weary pilgrim, Lord,
        Thy blessed summons waits.

THE WIND.

THE day is bright and clear, and clouds
    Of fleecy white arise
    Upon the perfect skies,
Mere playthings for the frolic wind,
Who for wild sport inclined,
    Out swiftly hies.

The dry leaves, sure, are sport enough
    For his wild frolic play;
    He scattereth them away,

And whirls them now, all round and round
Upon the sober ground,
The livelong day.

It makes me smile to watch the wind;
To-day he seems to be
Full of wild trickery;
Then sings himself to sleep—and you
Would think him dreaming, too,
So still he'll be.

He bends the tree-tops to and fro,
Then mounteth to the sky
To chase the clouds that lie
Like sleeping doves in the far West;
He wakes them from their rest,
And bids them fly.

Then far away he hies, to rouse
The placid wave, and creep
Over the tranquil deep;
Unquiet wind, I prithee rest
Upon the billows' gentle breast,
And sweetly sleep.

I hardly thought to write a verse
On such a fitful theme;
But it does ever seem
That nature brings unto my view
Some subject ever new
For my day-dream.

"Oh, Deck me not with Gems."

A SONG.

"Oh, deck me not with gems," she said,
"Oh, deck me not with gems;
I care not, for the princely light
Of jewelled diadems,
But give me flowers, the fresh, the fair,
Oh, give me fairy flowers
To deck my robe, to deck my hair,
From my own garden bowers."

"I know where gleam bright gems," she said,
"Bright gems in emerald set,
Fair rose-buds glistening in the dew,
And blue-eyed violet.

The jasmine stars, like orient pearls,
  I'll twine amid my hair,
And lilies of the valley sweet
  Upon my bosom wear."

"Nay, let me go," the fair girl said,
  "Nay, let me go and wreathe
A chaplet of my garden flowers,
  A coronet I'll weave.
You'll say 't is fairer far than gems,
  You'll say it is more fair,
My coronet of garden flowers,
  Than gems of beauty rare."

"I care not for bright gems," she said,
  "I care not for bright gems,
I care not for the jewelled light
  Of princely diadems.
My heart is with its early home,
  And its dear garden bowers;
Oh, deck me not with gems," she said,
  "But give me sweet home-flowers."

LISTEN.

LISTEN! Dost hear the voice
  Of wild bird on the air,
As up he soars, the merry heart!
  Rejoicing everywhere?

Dost love to hear the sound
  Of water's "silver feet,"
Tripping o'er pebbles round and smooth
  To music low and sweet;
The streamlet's careless tone,
  As he goes singing by,
'Mid flowers that peeping o'er the bank
  Their own bright faces spy?

Listen! Dost love to hear,
  At twilight's blessed hour,
The gentle lute steal o'er thy soul
  With its resistless power?
Dost love the human sound
  Of children at their play,
The merry laugh! the gleesome shout,
  Telling of life's young day,
Voices of friends around
  The consecrated hearth,
The pleasant word, the kind response
  The chastened quiet mirth?

Listen! Dost love to hear,
  At holy hush of even,
Voices of dear departed ones
  Now dwelling up in heaven?
The father's tone of love,
  The mother's gentle word,
Come back to us in later years
  The same that childhood heard!

Listen! To cheer thy heart,
These angels voices come,
Whispering, onward is thy path,
And upward is thy home.

To a Falling Leaf in September.

'Tis hardly time for thee to fade,
Why dost thou fall so fast;
As if a wintry blast
Had breathed upon thy pretty form?
The day is soft and warm,
And it may last.

September days are bright, I know,
And very warm and mild,
No tempest rude and wild

Has torn you from the parent bough.
Prithee why fallest thou
  To earth defiled ?

Alas ! alas ! a chilling frost,
  When all was clear and bright,
  Like to an elfin sprite,
Did come when all was calm and still
And touch you with a chill
  The other night.

And so you droop and die, alas !
  Though bright you look and gay ;
  And thus you pass away
Arrayed in colors manifold,
Scarlet most rich and gold
  To mock decay.

Ah ! I have known a maiden fair
  Touched by some hidden grief.
  Her mission here was brief,
For disappointment's chilling gloom
Did send her to the tomb
  Like this poor leaf.

And like this paltry thing did she,
  Thus in her early day,
  Look lovely in decay ;
The hectic flushed that maiden's cheek,
Who sadly fair and meek
  Did pass away.

THE RISEN LORD.

WITHOUT the sepulchre did Mary weep,
  Nor knew her risen Lord was standing near;
"Woman, why weepest thou? whom seekest thou?"
  In gentle accents sounded in her ear.
But still she weeps, nor lifts her drooping head,
  In grief intense, still mourning for her Lord.
Thinking some earthly friend is at her side,
  She heedeth not the Saviour's gentle word.

"Woman, why weepest thou? whom seekest thou?"
  The tearful Mary then sad answer made,
"If ye have borne my blessed Master hence,
  Oh, tell me where his precious form is laid!"
But Jesus chideth the sad weeper now;
  "Mary!" he saith; she lifts her tearful eyes.
"Rabboni! Master!" she astonished said—
  How great her joy, how gladdening her surprise.

Oh! oftentimes when sorrowful of heart,
  We see not that the risen Lord is near.
"Why weepest thou, sad Mary?" even now
  Falleth unheeded on the mourner's ear.
Let not our tears hide Jesus from our view,
  Nor let us see but earthly friends at hand;
But oh! like Mary, lift our eyes and see
  The risen Lord close at our side doth stand.

LINES

ON GAZING UPON THE LIFELESS FORM OF ONE MOST BELOVED.

THE setting is dark, and the gem is cold,
And mine eye is pained at the sight
Of the coffined jewel, that still to me
Is dearer than life and light.

The setting is dark, and the gem most fair,
For fairer ye ne'er have seen;
Though white, and still and lustreless now
Is the beautiful form I ween.

The setting is dark, and the gem most dear,
Oh, ye may not bear it away,
My life, my life—will ye heed it not!
Goes forth with that coffined clay.

The setting is dark, and the gem I prize,
But where is the casket meet,
That ye bear my treasure away from my sight,
With heavy reluctant feet?

Oh, the rich brown mould is the casket fair
With the sod for the casket lid,
And deep in its grave, far, far from my sight
My beautiful treasure is hid.

O God! to thy care this fair casket I yield,
With its pale gem of priceless worth;
Oh, guard it for me, with thy watchful eye,
Deep hid in the bosom of earth.

And at last bring it forth, from its secret place,
With beauty untarnished and bright,
And among thy fair jewels, dear Lord, make room
For my own in thy crown of light.

AUTUMN MUSINGS.

OH, they 're sweet, sad days, these autumn days,
They come o'er my heart like a sorrowful smile,
That would fain the careless eye beguile,
Though the heart is bursting with tears the while.
Oh, they 're sweet, sad days.

Oh, they 're sweet, sad times, these autumn times;
The heart goes forth to gather her flowers,
Though faded and sere are her beautiful bowers;
The heart's-ease springs up, though the storm cloud lowers:
Oh, they 're sweet, sad times.

Oh, they 're sweet, sad hours, these autumn hours;
The heart goes back to days long flown,
And counts her lost treasures one by one,
Yet grateful still for the mercies shown:
Oh, they 're sweet, sad hours.

Oh, they 're sweet, sad thoughts, these autumn tho'ts;
They tell of decay, but afar, afar,
The angel Hope, like the morning star,
Doth lead us on where our treasures are:
Oh, they 're sweet, sad thoughts.

Good Night! Little Daughter, Good Night!

Good night! little daughter, good night!
  Sleep sweetly! oh, quietly sleep.
Send down thy kind angels, our Father in heaven,
  A watch o'er the slumberer to keep.
Good night! little daughter, good night!

Good night! little daughter, good night!
  Dream sweetly—oh, quietly dream.
Send down blessed visions, our Father in heaven,
  Beneath her closed eyelids to gleam.
Good night! little daughter, good night!

Good night! little daughter, good night!
  Wake lightly—oh cheerfully wake;
With the clear morning light, our Father in heaven,
  Oh, break her light slumber—oh break.
Good night! little daughter, good night!

Good night! little daughter, good night!
  She is thine, blessed Jesus, is thine.
Oh, cease not to guard her, our Father in heaven,
  This treasure to thee I resign.
Good night! little daughter, good night!

FLOWER LESSONS.

"From the sweet floweret many a lesson learn
Of meek humility, of trusting love and faith."

THE sweetest flower, that in its humble pride
Contents itself to bloom in woodland shade,
To breathe its balmy influence far and wide,
To cheer its sisters in the mossy glade,

To open its sweet bosom to the sun,
To give its honey to the roving bee,
To close its pretty eye when day is done,
To open it when night's dark shadows flee,

To bloom its destined time, then meekly fade
  Without one thought of murmuring at its lot,
Knowing that He who delicately made
  Its fragile form, will sure forget it not,

Doth teach me many a lesson; oh, for trust
  Like thine, pale wilding thing, in God's kind care.
Knowing, like thee, sweet flower, his ways are just,
  His watchful love is o'er me everywhere.

I do not act my part like thee, fair thing,
  My heart does not expand with love for all;
How unlike thee, that sometimes I mistrust
  That God who heedeth when thy leaflets fall.

Sweet woodland flower, I'll come again, and learn
  A lesson from thy incense-breathing cells;
God made thee, and I'm sure I may not spurn
  To learn a lesson from thy simple bells.

A Hymn.

"Lord, what is man, that thou art mindful of him? and the son of man, that thou visitest him?"

"Thou art about my path, and about my bed, and spiest out all my ways."

Why art thou mindful, Lord, of me,
  That thus, with tender care
Thy watchful hand doth kindly guide
  My footsteps everywhere?

"About my path" thine eye of love
  Doth watch me lest I fall;
Thou knowest all my wanderings
  O Lord, and mark'st them all.

Thy hand supplieth me with food,
  My board by thee is spread;
And thou wouldst send me manna, Lord,
  Ere I should want for bread.
Thou sendest raiment too, that I
  May fear not winter's chill;
And thou dost temper the fierce wind,
  That I may feel no ill.

Thou visitest me on my couch,
  And sendest unto me
Most quiet sleep and pleasant dreams,
  That I refreshed may be.
Yes, every good and perfect gift,
  My Father, comes from thee;
But why art thou so mindful, Lord,
  Why dost thou visit me?

Hear what the Lord in love declares:
  "The humble and the meek,
And him who has no helper, I
  In mercy came to seek.

"He who doth ask in humble faith,
  Knowing he shall receive,
And trusting in my love alone,
  To him I love to give.

'T is that thou ownest 't is my hand,
And trustest all to me;
For this of thee I mindful am,
For this I visit thee."

Song.

AIR, "LONG, LONG AGO, LONG AGO."

SWEET, was the voice I delighted to hear
Long, long ago, long, long ago;
Welcome the tones that to me were so dear,
Long, long ago, long ago.
Fair was her cheek, as the rose's soft hue,
Dovelike and gentle her eyes' April-blue;
Kindest and purest the soul that beamed through,
Long, long ago, long ago.

Hushed was that voice I delighted to hear
Long, long ago, long, long ago;
Silent the tones that to me were most dear
Long, long ago, long ago;
Green is the turf now above her fair head,
Many and sorrowful tears have I shed
Over my cherished, my beautiful dead,
Long, long ago, long ago.

Yes, that dear voice I delighted to hear
Long, long ago, long, long ago;
Ever was soothing and sweet to my ear
Long, long ago, long ago.

Briefly to cheer me the loved one was given ;
Lonely is now my fireside at even,
For my sweet angel was taken to heaven
Long, long ago, long ago.

SINGING AWAY, LITTLE BIRDIE.

During a snowstorm in April, as I was looking from my window, I heard a robin singing very cheerily, high up in a maple-tree near the house, in spite of the snow and cold weather.

SINGING away, little birdie,
Singing high up in the tree ;
While snow-flakes are falling around thee,
And the north wind is blowing free :
Singing away, little birdie,
Though the branches are leafless and brown,
Rocking high up in the tree-top,
Thy sweet notes come cheerily down.

Singing away, little birdie!
  There is hope, and there's joy in thy song;
It says the cold winter is over,
  And that summer is coming ere long.
Singing away, little birdie,
  The bright days are coming to thee
When with mate and with feathery fledglings,
  Thou wilt find a soft nest in this tree.

Singing away, little birdie!
  Our Father, oh, teach me to praise,
When clouds and thick darkness are round me,
  And sorrow o'ershadows my days.
Thy lesson, I'm learning, sweet bird,
  As thou singest high up in the tree,
Of faith and of love for "our Father,"
  Who careth for thee and for me.

Sad Moments.

Who hath not her sad moments, when the heart,
Wearied with life and sighing for its rest,
Returns, like wearied birds to their own nest,
Back to itself, and quietly apart
From busy life and folly's crowded mart,
Sweetly reposes, while the God of peace
Doth from above a heavenly calm impart,
And all sad weariness and troubles cease.

Oh, grant me ever, Lord, in my sad hours,
When wearied with the tumult and the strife
Of ever-changing, ever-restless life,
When my bowed head, like a frost-stricken flower,
Can feel no joy in sunshine or in shower,
Then in my weakness to find strength in thee.
Thou Lord, alone, with thy almighty power,
Canst comfort the sad heart. Oh, grant to me
How dark soe'er the day of sorrow lower,
Shining o'er all thy wondrous love to see.

LOST AND WON.

Lost the freshness of life's morning,
  Lost the tints of rosy light,
Which at daylight's perfect dawning,
  Covers all with glory bright.
Lost the golden locks which shaded
  Brow so fair and eyes so blue,
And the happy smile has faded,
  Round those lips of rosy hue.
      I have lost, but I have won.

Lost, the kind oblivious sleeping
  Which enshrouds the little child,
With the holy angels keeping
  Saintly watches, calm and mild.

Lost the dreams of sunny hours,
  Where no sorrow dare intrude,
Lost the dreams of love and flowers,
  Of the beautiful and good.
          I have lost, but I have won.

Lost, oh, worst of all the losses!
  Lost the childlike earnest faith,
Loving on, 'mid joys and crosses,
  Thankful still for all it hath.
I have lost youth's simple pleasures,
  All have withered, one by one;
But, oh, blessings without measure,
          I have lost, but I have won.

I have won, through earnest striving,
  Guerdons, above all the loss,
Hopes once faded, now reviving,
  Clinging round the sacred cross;
Sorrow pale hath been my teacher,
  Hopes bereft my gentle friends,
Graves of the loved my silent preachers,
  Where with dust dust sadly blends.
          I have lost, but I have won.

I have won through tribulation
  Title to a heavenly home,
Working out my own salvation,
  Through the blood of Christ alone.

Oh, my future brightest seemeth,
  Seen by faith instead of sight,
While celestial splendor beameth
  On my darkness from that light!
            I have lost, but I have won.

I have won bright hopes immortal
  Of a heaven of peace and rest,
And am drawing near the portal
  As a kindly bidden guest.
Lost and won! O earth! O heaven!
  Hark! I list the angels' strain
Floating out from that fair haven:
  "Small the loss, and great the gain!"
            I have lost, but I have won.

THE LATTER RAIN.

How it rains now, pouring, pouring,
  From the thick and clouded sky;
Now in showers, now dull and slowly,
  Fall the raindrops from on high,
Making the fresh grass look greener,
  Though all else is dull and gray,
Still the raindrops are a blessing
  To the bright green fields alway.
            Pouring, pouring.

How it rains now, soaking, soaking,
In the dull and dusty earth,
Filling up the little fountains,
Giving mimic rivers birth.
Fill up, springs, before cold winter
Binds the outside earth in chains;
Close within her bosom warmly
Hoards she up the autumn rains.
Soaking, soaking.

How it rains now, dripping, dripping,
From the houses, from the sheds,
From umbrellas, wide extended
To protect the travellers' heads.
With warm smiles man greets his neighbor,
Passes on, and smiles again;
All feel cheerful and gladhearted,
Grateful for the latter rain.
Dripping, dripping.

How it rains now, dripping, pouring,
Soaking fast into the ground,
While I at my chamber window
Cast a grateful look around
At the green grass, and the streamlets,
And the people passing by,
For the raindrops, like all blessings,
Are a gift from God on high.
Falling, falling.

Angel Voices.

I hear them, oh, I hear them,
  When I am sad and lone,
And my heart would count her treasures
  Of the dear ones that are gone.
My tearful eyes in sadness
  Look round for them in vain,
And my trembling lip scarce utters
  "They will never come again!"
And then upon the silence
  Those angel voices come,
And bring my wandering spirit back
  To scenes of love and home.

My mother's words so gentle,
  In accents soft I hear:
My father's tones of kindly love
  Fall on my listening ear.
And children's voices, like the birds',
  I hear so soft and sweet,
And the laughter from their merry hearts,
  And the tread of little feet.
The silken curls of childhood,
  The eyes of heaven's own blue;
The elder and the later friends,
  The warm, the tried, the true,
I hear them, oh, I hear them,

And I fancy they are near,
The friends so loved and cherished,
The treasured and the dear.

I hear them, oh, I hear them,
Nor is their mission vain,
They come to wipe the tearful eyes,
And ease the heart of pain;
They come, in accents gentle
To tell us not to fear,
For great the clouds of witnesses
Encompassing us here.
To aid our weak endeavors,
To comfort us they come,
To point us from our earthly joys
Unto our heavenly home.

A VALENTINE,

SENT TO JOHNNY L——, AGED TWO YEARS.

Of all the cupids, in my eyes,
There 's none with little Johnny vies;
So fat, so rosy, and so fair,
I must his precious worth declare.

The violet's cup is not so blue
As Johnny's eyes of azure hue,
With fringèd lids to ope and close,
Like petals of the maiden rose.

No fragrant flower from sunny south
Is sweet as Johnny's little mouth,
Where pearls within their coral bed
Gleam out amid the rubies red.

No shining silk so soft and fair
As Johnny's pretty flaxen hair,
As o'er his shoulders, broad and white,
It falls in threads of golden light.

No music makes my heart rejoice
Like Johnny's pleasant little voice;
No song of waters half so sweet
As Johnny's tripping little feet.

No other boy will we compare
To Johnny boy—so fat and fair;
Good-natured all the livelong day,
And full of frolic, fun, and play.

My muse thus Johnny's praises sings,
A little cupid without wings;
And if the rogue will not decline,
Will take him for her Valentine.

The First Violet.

'Twas a little thing; and all alone
By a bubbling spring it stood,
Where the sun shone down through the leafless trees
Of a grand and silent wood.

'T was a little thing, with a mild blue eye,
And fair and frail to see,
As shrinking it hid itself, alone
Beneath the tall fir-tree.

But it had a pleasant, hopeful look,
And spoke of summer hours,
When from the chilly and dark brown earth
Would spring forth many flowers.

It seemed like a herald, sent to say
That spring was very near,
With flowers and songs and pleasant things
The sombre earth to cheer.

I gathered that violet lone and small,
  And its breath was fragrant and sweet;
And I bore it home through the long high-road,
  And the dusty city street.

And now it stands in my quiet room
  Close by me, while I write;
And it gladdens my heart to have it so near,
  A creature so gentle and bright.

How kindly hath God in his love attuned
  My heart with its thousand strings,
To a kindly love for the lone wild-flower
  That stood by the woodland springs.

And how the hand of the Lord is traced
  In forming this violet fair,
Which stood alone in the silent wood
  In the chilly evening air.

COULDEST NOT THOU WATCH ONE HOUR?

MARK 14:37.

COULD'ST not thou watch one hour?
  My Saviour said to me,
As lone and sorrowful he prayed
  In dark Gethsemane;

One hour this night of gloom,
While I apart shall pray:
Father, if 'tis thy will, this cup
Untasted take away!

Could'st thou not watch one hour,
That darkest hour of all,
When on the cross in agony
Upon "my God" I call?

Could'st thou not watch one hour,
Sitting by Joseph's tomb,
Where cold in death thy Master lies
In loneliness and gloom?

Oh, hadst thou watched one hour
In sorrow's dreary night,
Thou wouldst have seen the glorious burst
Of resurrection's light.

Dear Lord, my faith is weak,
My fears are weaker still;
Teach me to watch and wait with thee,
And *do* thy blessed will.

Oh, wilt thou watch with me
In my dark hours of woe,
And to thy humble suppliant, Lord,
Thy boundless mercy show?

With me, through toil and care—
  With me, through death's dark night—
With me, to hail th' eternal day,
  The resurrection's light.

Waiting for the Morning.

"I'm waiting for the morning,"
  The languid sufferer said,
As worn with pain and weariness
  She lay upon her bed.
"I'm looking at the eastern skies,
  To watch the coming dawn;
Oh, give me patience, blessèd Lord,
  While waiting for the morn.

"I'm waiting for the morning,
  To-night I cannot sleep;
I'm listening for the first bird-note
  To break the silence deep.
I'm watching for the twitter
  On leafy bough and spray,
And praying still for patience
  While waiting for the day.

"I'm waiting for the morning;
  I long to see the sun
Come forth in glory golden,
  His daily course to run;

To watch him from the hill-tops
  Dispelling shades of night,
And beaming on my patient eyes
  While waiting for the light."

Thus "waiting for the morning"
  The weary sufferer lay,
And saw the golden glories
  Of a never-ending day;
While gazing at the eastern skies,
  Before the early dawn,
Her Saviour sent and called her home
  While waiting for the morn.

My Cross.

It is not heavy, agonizing woe,
  Bearing me down with hopeless, crushing weight;
No ray of comfort in the gathering gloom—
  A heart bereaved, a household desolate.

It is not sickness, with its withering hand,
  Keeping me low upon a couch of pain,
Longing each morning for the weary night,
  At night for weary day to come again.

It is not poverty, with chilling blast,
  The sunken eye, the hunger-wasted form,
My dear ones perishing for lack of bread,
  With no safe shelter from the winter's storm.

It is not slander, with her evil tongue;
'T is no "presumptuous sin" against my God;
Not reputation lost, nor friends betrayed—
That such is not my cross, I thank thee, Lord.

Mine is a daily cross of petty care
Of little duties pressing on my heart,
Of little troubles hard to meet and bear,
Of inward struggles, overcome in part.

My feet are weary in their daily rounds,
My heart is weary of its daily care,
My sinful nature often doth rebel;
I pray for grace my *daily* cross to bear.

It is not heavy, Lord; yet oft I pine:
It is not heavy, *but 't is ever here;*
By night and day, each hour my cross I bear;
I dare not lay it down—thou'st placed it there.

I dare not lay it down; I only ask,
That taking up my daily cross, I may
Follow my Master humbly, step by step,
Through clouds and darkness unto perfect day.

THINE FOR EVER.

THINE for ever! thine for ever!
What to me is chance or change?
Can the love I once have plighted
Ever to my heart be strange?

Thine for ever! So I whispered
  When thy lips first spoke of love.
Thine for ever! though now severed—
  I on earth and thou above.

Thine for ever! was thy promise;
  "Not till death us part," was mine.
Through this life, and still for ever,
  Thou art mine and I am thine.

Thine for ever! What though anguish,
  Oh, most deep, did rend my heart,
When on earth our bliss was severed,
  And I saw thy life depart!

Saw thine eyes—most tender gazers—
  Close in death while fixed on mine!
Felt *my* life was fast departing
  While I, trembling, watched for thine!

Saw thy form borne sadly from me,
  Laid beneath the grassy sod;
Knew my eyes no more would greet thee,
  Till we meet before our God!

What though many suns have lingered
  O'er thy lonely grass-clad bed!
What though nights and days have found me
  Weeping o'er my blessed dead!

Thine for ever! still for ever!
  Oh, no death can part us twain.
Thine on earth, and thine in heaven.
  Blessed thought—we meet again.

Meet! We never yet have parted.
  Thy dear form is lost to sight;
But the hearts which God united
  Death can never disunite.

Thine for ever! Others whisper
  Words of love into my ear;
Know they not the deathless feeling
  Which will ever linger here?

Know they not that love like ours,
  On through life and death the same,
Knows no change? that earthly sorrows
  Cannot quench the sacred flame?

Thine for ever! Soon I meet thee,
  Still thine own, as thou art mine;
Meet thee, never more to sever—
  Still thine own—for ever thine.

"It Hath Ceased to Beat."

It hath ceased to beat! it hath ceased to beat!
  That heart—that heart.
It hath throbbed with pleasure, it hath throbbed with
  pain:
But, alas, it never will throb again.

Stilly, oh, stilly, beneath the shroud,
Icy and cold—oh, icy and cold,
That heart that was so warm of old.
It hath beat against mine,
Oh, oftentime.
I place my hand on the lifeless clay,
And turn, oh, mournfully, away,
When I think of the heart in that quiet breast
That lieth so silently in its long rest.

They have ceased to move, they have ceased to move,
Those hands—those hands.
They have toiled in pleasure, they 've toiled in pain,
But, alas, they never can move again.
Stilly, oh, stilly, upon the shroud,
Folded so meekly, but stark and cold,
Those hands that were active and warm of old.
They have claspèd mine,
Oh oftentime.
I press those hands to my aching heart,
And, weeping, I turn with a tearful start,
As I think that the coffin will over them press,
And I shall be left in my loneliness.

They have ceased to move, they have ceased to move,
Those lips—those lips.
They have cheered me in sorrow, they 've cheered me in pain,
But, alas, they never will speak again.
Cold and pale, oh, pale and cold,
Those lips that were rosy and warm of old!

They have pressed against mine,
Oh, oftentime.
I touch them now, but I shudder with fear.
O Death, thy signet most surely is here;
And I turn aside. Ah, well-a-day!
I dare not look on my coffined clay.

It hath passed away, it hath passed away,
That life—that life.
It hath passed to regions of upper day,
To dwell with God and his saints alway.
Stilly, oh, stilly, in garments white,
She glideth at peace in those mansions fair,
Where the pure in heart and the angels are.
Sad heart of mine,
Oh, oftentime
Follow the saint to her blessed home,
Where tears of anguish can never come;
And turn from thy dust, though treasured and blest,
To the home of the ransomed, the heaven of rest.

MY DEAD.

THROUGH the long village street,
Trodden by many feet,
Past pleasant homes and marts of busy trade,
Up the sweet "Woodbine road,"
By orchards with their load
Of ruddy fruit or rose-hued blossoms' shade.

On through the rustic gate,
At early morn and late,
The dew, like tears, lies on each blade of grass;
The grass that grows on graves,
And o'er them gently waves,
Whisp'ring its tale to me as on I pass.

Up the broad gravelled grade,
To narrow paths inlaid
With grassy steps and slopes of sunny green,
With gentlest steps I tread;
I am coming to my dead,
Whose headstone by that turf-clad mound is seen.

Only the name and age,
Upon that marble page,
Tells to the world the story of my dead,
But to my aching heart,
The life-long tale impart
Of him who slumbers in that narrow bed.

Down in that grave so deep,
As if in pleasant sleep,
With folded hands and meekly closèd eyes—
Oh, in that lowly grave,
My noble and my brave,
My love, my all, in his last slumber lies.

I stood beside my dead,
When holy prayers were said,
And earth to earth and dust to dust were given;
But my dear Lord stood near,
With words of solemn cheer,
The Resurrection and the Life from heaven.

And now, in faith and trust,
I watch this sacred dust,
My priceless treasure, in its lowly bed;
And He who never sleeps
A tireless vigil keeps:
To his unslumbering care I yield my dead.

ANGEL CHILDREN.

TWO LITTLE GRAVES.

SIDE by side they 're sweetly sleeping
  Little loved ones, early blest,
Free from care and pain and sorrow.
  Oh, rejoice, they are at rest.

One whose timid little footfall
  Now we listen for in vain,
And whose voice, like bird-notes ringing,
  Never will be heard again.
Her blue eyes, like angels' beaming,
  Nevermore will meet our own.
Oh, her absence makes most dreary
  Our once cheerful, happy home.

And the other little sleeper,
  For a shorter season given,
Like a sunbeam sent to cheer us,
  Quickly taken back to heaven.

Vainly will her mother seek her;
  Vacant is her cradle-bed.
Lovely infant, in the graveyard
  Low is laid thy little head.

But the graveyard, oh, the graveyard!
  Let us turn our thoughts away,
Looking upward, looking upward,
  Into realms of cloudless day.
Side by side, in heaven's bright regions,
  Two sweet angels sing and soar,
Welcomed by the host of heaven,
  There to dwell for evermore.

Side by side, these little loved ones
  Hover round you night and day,
List your weeping and your sighing,
  And methinks these words they say:
"Did you know how blest and happy
  Angels are, ye would not mourn
That to join that band in heaven
  Your belovèd ones have gone.

"Side by side, in garments spotless,
  Angels twain, how blest are we!
Kindly Jesus Christ did call us:
  'Little children, come to me!'
Soon the Lord will call you heavenward;
  Side by side we then will come,
Stand to greet you at the portals
  Of our everlasting home."

Behold, He Sleepeth.

I entered in a darkened room,
  The chamber of the dead;
Behold, a child most sweetly fair
In little shroud of white lay there,
Holy and calm his features were,
  Though light and life had fled,
And tearful eyes did vigil keep;
No more he'll wake, no more he'll weep,
  Sweetly asleep, sweetly asleep.

I entered in the graveyard lone;
  With sad and solemn tread
They laid that angel-child to rest,
Calmly, within the earth's cold breast,
And mourners hushed their wailing, lest
  They wake the silent dead;
Down in the grave, quiet and deep,
No more to sorrow or to weep,
  Sweetly asleep, sweetly asleep.

Methought I entered in the land
  Of heavenly peace and joy,
And lo, beside still waters I
A lovely angel did descry
Slumbering most calmly, quietly;
  That angel was your boy.

And seraphs' eyes bright vigils keep ;
No more he 'll sorrow, no more weep.
  Sweetly asleep, sweetly asleep.

By faith I entered in the fold
  Which the great Shepherd tendeth :
Lo, in his arms a lamb most fair
Safely the Shepherd guardeth there.
A "little one," with watchful care,
  He loveth and defendeth :
Then for your lost one do not weep.
Your little lamb the Lord will keep.
  Sweetly asleep, sweetly asleep.

Our Lamb.

Take away the little baby,
  Folded in his garments white,
Place him in the rosewood casket.
  Close the lid upon him tight ;
Throw the pall upon the coffin,
  Bear our little one away ;
Leave me in my quiet chamber,
  We have lost our lamb to-day.

Bear the casket and its jewel
  Out beneath the open sky ;
Dust to dust—our little treasure
  With its mother-earth must lie.

Heap the sod upon the coffin,
  Hide our darling quite away;
Leave me in my quiet chamber,
  We have lost our lamb to-day.

Let him sleep on, while the daisies
  Bloom upon the grassy sod;
Leave him there, our fairest flower,
  Leave our darling with his God.
Very lonely, sad, and heart-sick,
  On my bed I weep and pray;
Leave me in my quiet chamber,
  We have lost our lamb to-day.

Only three short weeks I had him,
  Folded in my arms of love;
Then the heavenly Shepherd called him
  To that other fold above.
Oh, I know our child is safest,
  Borne on angel wings away,
Yet my tears are falling, falling,
  For we 've lost our lamb to-day.

Bear him, angels, far above us,
  To the regions of the blest;
No more pain, no sin, no sorrow—
  Safe within the fold of rest.
Throbbing heart-aches, tears of anguish,
  Let me banish you away;
Oh, rejoice! though sick and lonely,
  Heaven has gained our lamb to-day.

God, in his good time, will send us
Blessèd comforts from above;
He who wept o'er Laz'rus sleeping,
Looks on us with pitying love.
Little lamb, in Jesus' keeping,
Christ himself calls thee away;
Heavenly Shepherd, gently, gently
Guide our little lamb to-day.

Where, Where art Thou Gone, Little Baby?

Where, where art thou gone, little baby?
Thy voice in its gladness has ceased;
I hear not the delicate tread
Of thy soft foot; they say thou art dead,
And sweetly art sleeping in peace;
Gone sweetly to sleep, little baby—
They say thou art sleeping in peace.

Where, where art thou gone, little baby?
Where's the sweet sunny light of thine eye?
Thy beautiful face ever smiling,
The heart of thy mother beguiling,
In the damp, narrow grave thou dost lie,
In the grave, in the grave, little baby,
In the damp, narrow grave thou dost lie.

That small, but that beautiful garment
Of perfect and well-finished clay

Thou hast gently cast off, and ascending
To regions of glory unending,
Thy spirit in light is arrayed;
Clothed in light, clothed in light, little baby,
Thy spirit in light is arrayed.

We shall meet thee again, little baby;
For God, in his wonderful love,
Has told us, sweet baby, of heaven,
Where the sinless and sin-forgiven
Shall meet in his kingdom above;
Then above, then above, little baby,
God grant we may meet thee above.

LITTLE NANNIE,

WHO DIED ——, AGED THREE YEARS AND EIGHT MONTHS.

SAFE, safe within the fold, Nannie,
Within the Saviour's fold;
Jesus, the gentle Shepherd, now
His little lamb doth hold.
He'll lead thee forth, dear Nannie,
Where the "still waters" glide,
And 'mid "green pastures" fresh and fair
Thy tiny feet will guide.

Our eyes are dimmed with weeping
As we think of Nannie gone,
The light of all our hearts and homes,
The little precious one.

The music of those little feet,
That brightly-beaming eye,
The joyous laugh, the merry voice,
Will live in memory.

Her little journey over
Before the heat of day,
In early dawn and freshness
She sweetly passed away.
No thorns had pierced those little feet
As o'er life's path she trod;
Unwearied, she has reached the goal,
And stands before her God.

We cannot cease our weeping;
But we will meekly bow,
And bless the Hand that chastens us,
And laid our treasure low.
Upward we lift our tear-dimmed eyes,
And thee, dear lamb, behold,
Oh, safe within the fold, Nannie,
Within the Saviour's fold.

One Little Boy is Missing.

One little boy is missing
From the village green to-night,
One voice of merry laughter,
One footstep quick and light.

Playmates are sadly turning
  From their pleasant sports away,
For a darling boy is missing,
  They have no heart to play.

One little chair is empty
  In a cheerful cottage-home,
As round the table gather
  The inmates one by one.
And parents, humbly kneeling
  Before the throne of grace,
Pause with a sobbing heart-ache,
  Missing one upturned face.

One bounding step is missing,
  As up the chamber stair
The little ones are climbing,
  After the evening prayer :

And one small bed untumbled,
With pillow soft and white,
For one dear child is missing
From the children-band to-night.

One voice has joined the choir
In the angel-song above,
One spirit bright and beautiful
Sings of redeeming Love
Look upward, tearful mourners,
And wipe your tears away,
Though a darling boy is missing
From your cottage-home to-day.

OUR NELLIE.

I MISS no less thy sunny head,
Close nestling to my heart at even,
When thinking of the golden crown
Thou wearest in the courts of heaven.
I miss no less thy treasured form,
That was our joy, our heart's delight,
When thinking thou art "clothed upon,"
And walkest with the saints in white.

I miss no less thy tiny hands,
So busy in their active play,
When thinking of the harp of gold
Thou tunest to angelic lay.

I miss no less the fairy fall
  Of little feet upon the stair,
When thinking that thou roamest now
  In heavenly regions, bright and fair.

I miss no less thy blessèd voice,
  Which, like a bird's, was full of song.
When thinking that before God's throne
  Thou singest with the angel throng;
The sunny head, the treasured form,
  The voice of music to my ear,
The little feet, the tiny hands,
  Are still most dear, are still most dear.

Oh, we have blest assurances
  That with dear Nellie "all is well;"
That she, dear lamb, is safe with God;
  But of our anguish who can tell?
The lonely hearth, the lonely home,
  The lonely night, the lonely day:
God comfort us, God comfort us!
  Is all our broken hearts can say.

Baby Coming Home.

Baby has come home again,
But we listen, ah, in vain,
  For the sound of little feet,
  For the voice of music sweet,
  For the thousand cunning ways
  Mothers love so much to praise;

For the presence bright and fair,
Like a sunbeam everywhere—
Yes, we listen, ah, in vain,
Though baby has come home again.

Baby has come home again,
But our tears fall as the rain ;
Bear her gently ; she 's asleep ;
Do not break the slumber deep :
Look ! within the casket fair
Lies our priceless treasure there ;
Little foot and hand are still,
Pulseless heart no more will thrill.
Sleeping—no more tears or pain,
Darling will not wake again ;
Pure white flowers are round her spread,
Fairest flower—the baby dead :
Oh, our tears fall as the rain,
Though baby has come home again.

God has taken baby home ;
Father, mother, will you come
And meet her on the heavenly shore,
When life's weary day is o'er ?
See ! she 's with the angel throng ;
Hark ! she sings the angel's song.
Precious treasure ! oh, how blest
In the Saviour's arms to rest :
"Suffer the little one to come,"
Thus Jesus called your darling home.

The Little, Lonely Grave.

Oh, very sad it makes me feel,
Thus leaving these dear scenes,
The home of many happy days
And many sunny dreams;
And friends whose love around my heart
Is shed like holy beams.

But 't is not for my friends or home
For whom I linger still:
Oh, no—a little, lonely grave
Beneath yon gentle hill
Calls up these tears and broken sobs,
Albeit against my will.

A little grave! the stranger's eye
Would hardly note the spot;
So unobtrusive is its form,
At them I wonder not;
Yet to some hearts, I know full well
'T will never be forgot.

For, oh! 't is everything to me,
This little mound of green,
Though now the little form beneath
Is crumbling dust, I ween.
Yet, oh! most precious doth the dust
Of such a treasure seem.

Thoughts of that little, lonely grave
Beneath the green hill shade
Come over me with anguish now
As when it first was made,
And earth to earth and dust to dust
Their solemn sound conveyed.

For there, within, my first-born child
Was laid in slumber fair;
So life-like that I did mistrust
That death was imaged there.
They heaped the dark mould o'er his head
And said a holy prayer.

And there he sleeps, so wonder not
That thus my tears will flow;
That little grave, that lonely grave
To leave unguarded so,
While far away from these dear scenes
I must for ever go.

Who'll guard that little hillock green,
The tombstone at its head;
That little, lonely, cherished grave
That holds my cherished dead?
May God and angels watch above
My sleeping infant's bed.

Full well I know the Saviour says,
"Of such my kingdom is;"
I know the spirit of my child

Is robed in perfect bliss.
Thrice wretched, ah! indeed were I,
Had *He* not told me this.

But, oh! that little, lonely grave
Is all that I can see
Of the sweet form that was the joy
Of all my life to me.
Will God forgive, that mortals thus
Worship mortality?

UNDER THE SNOW.

BEAUTIFUL things lie hidden
Under the snow;
Tulips and daffodils sleeping,
Myrtles with broad leaves are creeping,
And blue-eyed forget-me-nots peeping,
Under the snow.

Beautiful things lie hidden
Under the snow;
The crocus and dear little daisies,
And arbutus, twining in mazes,
Its sweet-scented flow'rets upraises
Under the snow.

Beautiful things lie hidden
Under the snow;

But they will awake in the morning,
When Spring with warm sunshine is dawning
They will peep out from under the awning
Under the snow.

Our dear little Alice lies hidden
Under the snow;
The angels their kind watch are keeping
O'er our beautiful treasure safe sleeping;
No pain and no sorrow or weeping
Under the snow.

Yes, beautiful Alice lies sleeping
Under the snow;
But she will awake in the morning,
At the bright resurrection-day dawning,
No more to lie down midst our mourning,
Under the snow.

Angel Children.

Two darling little children
Came to my mind to-day,
Who once were with us, long ago,
And then were called away.
They now are angel-children,
Before the great white throne.
They sing the praises of their God,
Who took them for his own.

One—black-eyed little Bessie—
So full of life and glee,
So merry-hearted all day long,
And gay as gay could be.
Three little years she lived on earth;
And now, above the sky,
Among the angel-children, she
Now dwells in bliss on high.

And Kate, our little treasure,
With eyes of tender blue,
And silken curls so shining,
And lips of rosy hue.
Close, close beside dear Bessie
Her little grave was made,
And green the broad-leaved prairie-grass
Over their heads doth wave.

And now two little angels
Seem right before my eyes,
Looking upon me from their homes
Of glory in the skies.
No sickness now, no sighing,
No grief, nor any pain.
Safe! safe! Oh, who would call them back
To live on earth again?

Thank God for little children,
Who need such tender care.
The Saviour calls them: "Come to me
My own the children are."

Thank God for angel children,
  Bidding us look above,
And listen to the heavenly choirs
  Singing redeeming love.

Baby Alice.

Art sleeping, baby Alice,
  Upon thy cradle-bed?
Oh, fair the pure white flowers
  And violets round thee spread.
How stilly lie thy folded hands,
  How blue thy half-closed eye!
Art sleeping, baby Alice—
  Sleeping so silently?

Art sleeping, pretty Alice?
  We call to thee in vain:
Most desolate our hearth and hearts,
  Oh, wake, and come again!
We miss thy tottling footstep;
  We miss thy laughing tone,
Thy thousand pretty winning ways:
  Are they for ever gone?

Art sleeping, little Alice?
  The holy prayer was said,
And—earth to earth and dust to dust—
  We laid thee with the dead.

Gently we laid our treasure down,
  In faith and holy trust,
And sweetly in the green graveyard
  Doth sleep thy precious dust.

Art sleeping, angel Alice?
  Upon thy Saviour's breast,
Safe, safe within his precious fold
  Our little lamb doth rest.
Oh, keep her, blessed Jesus!
  Our sacred treasure keep,
Till we like angel Alice,
  In thee shall fall asleep!

www.ingramcontent.com/pod-product-compliance
Lightning Source LLC
Chambersburg PA
CBHW032358280326
41935CB00008B/625